# Japanese Blossoms

## *an Adult Coloring Book*

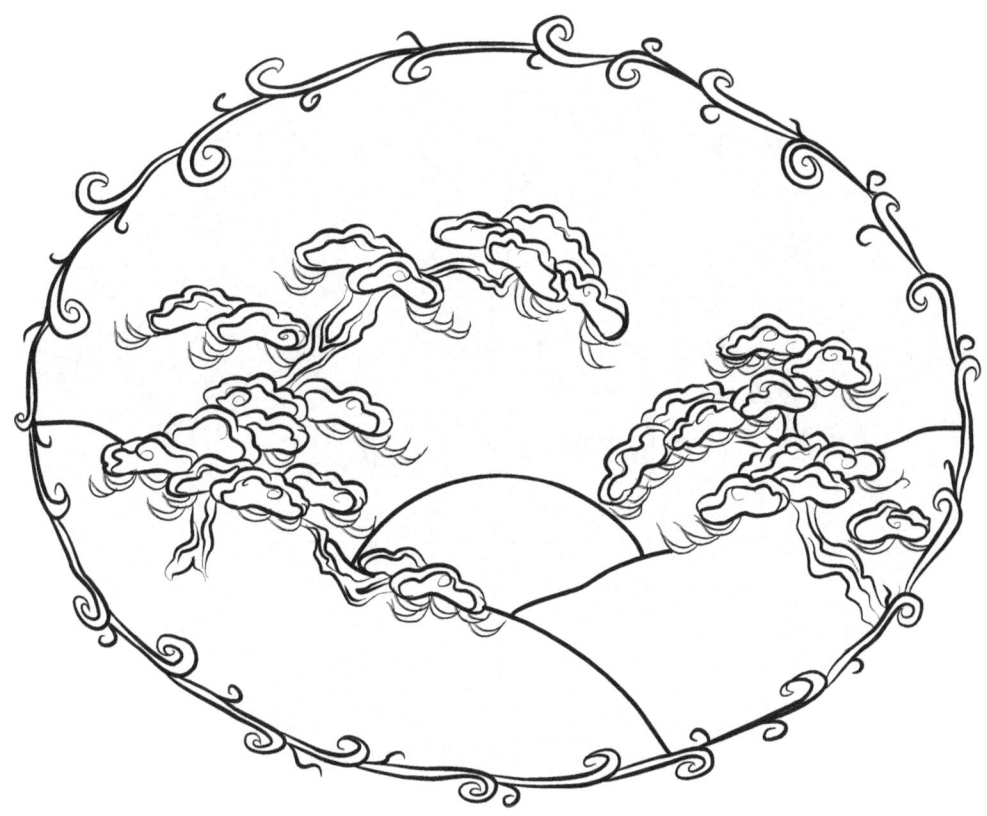

by Tes Scholtz

*Artwork Anywhere*™

Color this!
Yours could be our new facebook cover photo!
Get more info and download printable copies at
ArtworkAnywhere.com/fb

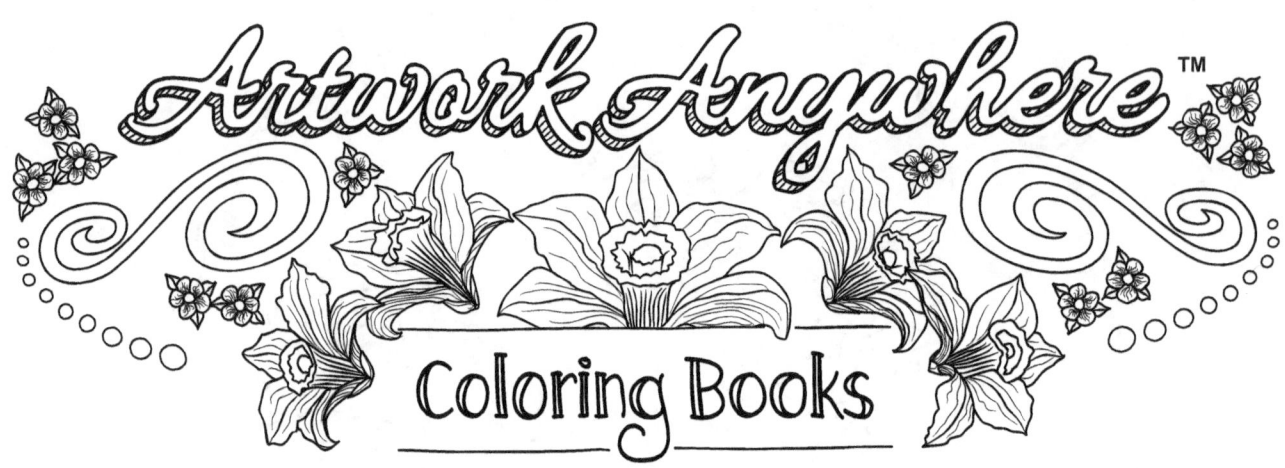

Cover: The front and back cover were designed and colored by Tes Scholtz.
Hand coloring was done with Recollections™ Signature™ Masterpiece II Markers.

# Japanese Blossoms
## an Adult Coloring Book

### by Tes Scholtz

*Artwork Anywhere* ™

*Japanese Blossoms* adult coloring book features 25 hand drawn illustrations inspired by timeless Japanese designs. Flower blossoms are layered with bamboo and geometric patterns, then sprinkled with birds and butterflies. Fanciful shapes and whimsical scenes make these pages a delight to color. Antique Japanese designs in the public domain were used for reference and inspiration.

*"I was so inspired by the creative layering of shapes and patterns in the old Japanese designs I found. I felt they needed to be made fresh and shared with you. I hope you find them as intriguing as I do!" ~Tes*

Use colored pencils, crayons, inks, gel pens, markers, whatever you want, or mix it up and use them all! There are no rules. There are suggestions, though: Some markers and paints may bleed through the pages. To avoid damaging other pages, use a barrier sheet between pages, or remove the page from the book before coloring.

All of my coloring books are printed single-sided, so you don't have to worry about colors showing through the back side, or smudging against each other face-to-face. Plus, no more deciding which side you like better if you want to remove it from the book.

 *ArtworkAnywhere.com*

Be sure to check out ArtworkAnywhere.com for our latest coloring books, plus updates, contests, and exclusive free coloring pages!

We love to see your work! Please share your favorite colorings, so we can show it off! Please visit ArtworkAnywhere.com/social to see where we are on social media.

Do you have questions, criticism, compliments, ideas? Send your thoughts to: suggestions@artworkanywhere.com

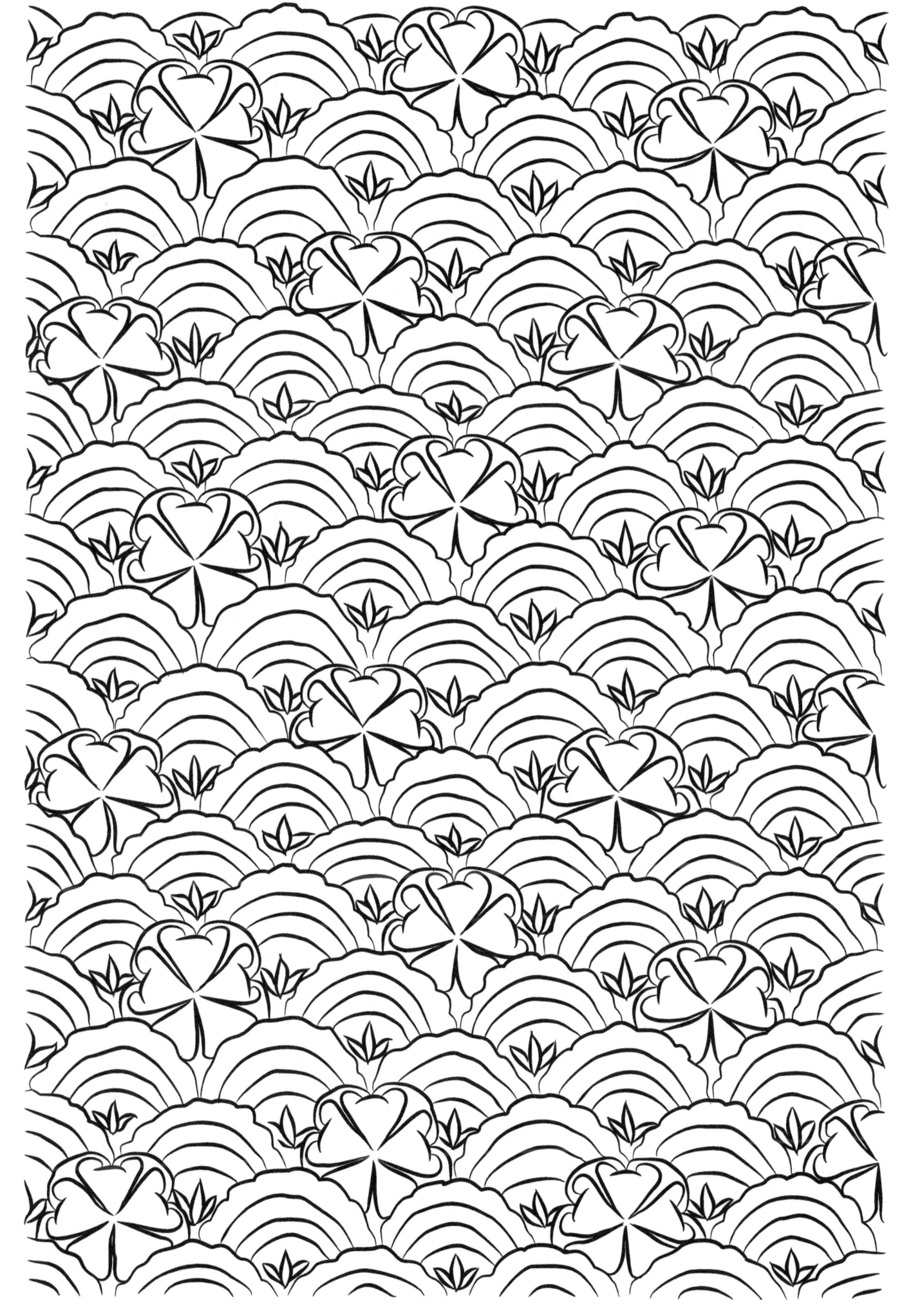

ArtworkAnywhere.com

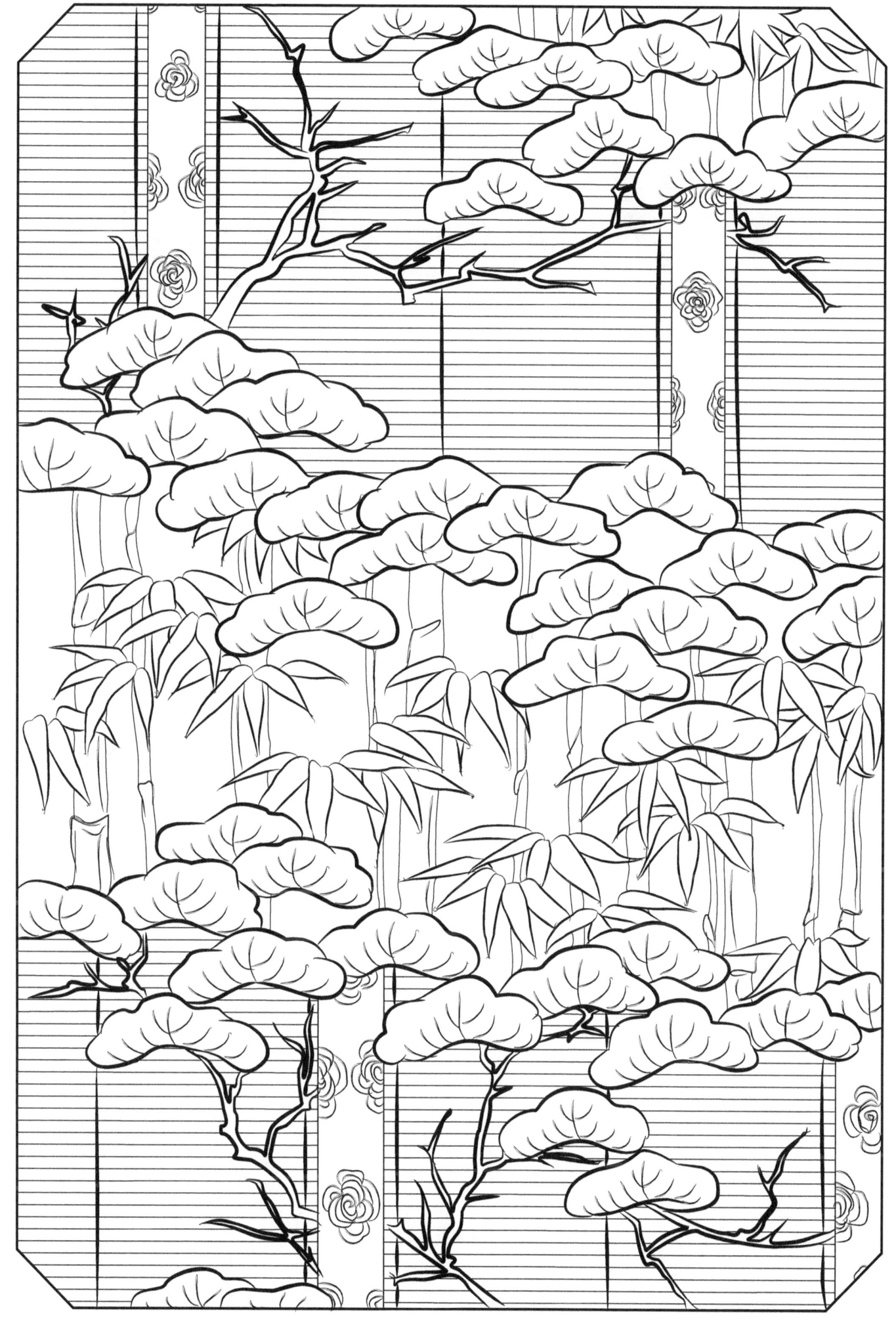

ArtworkAnywhere.com

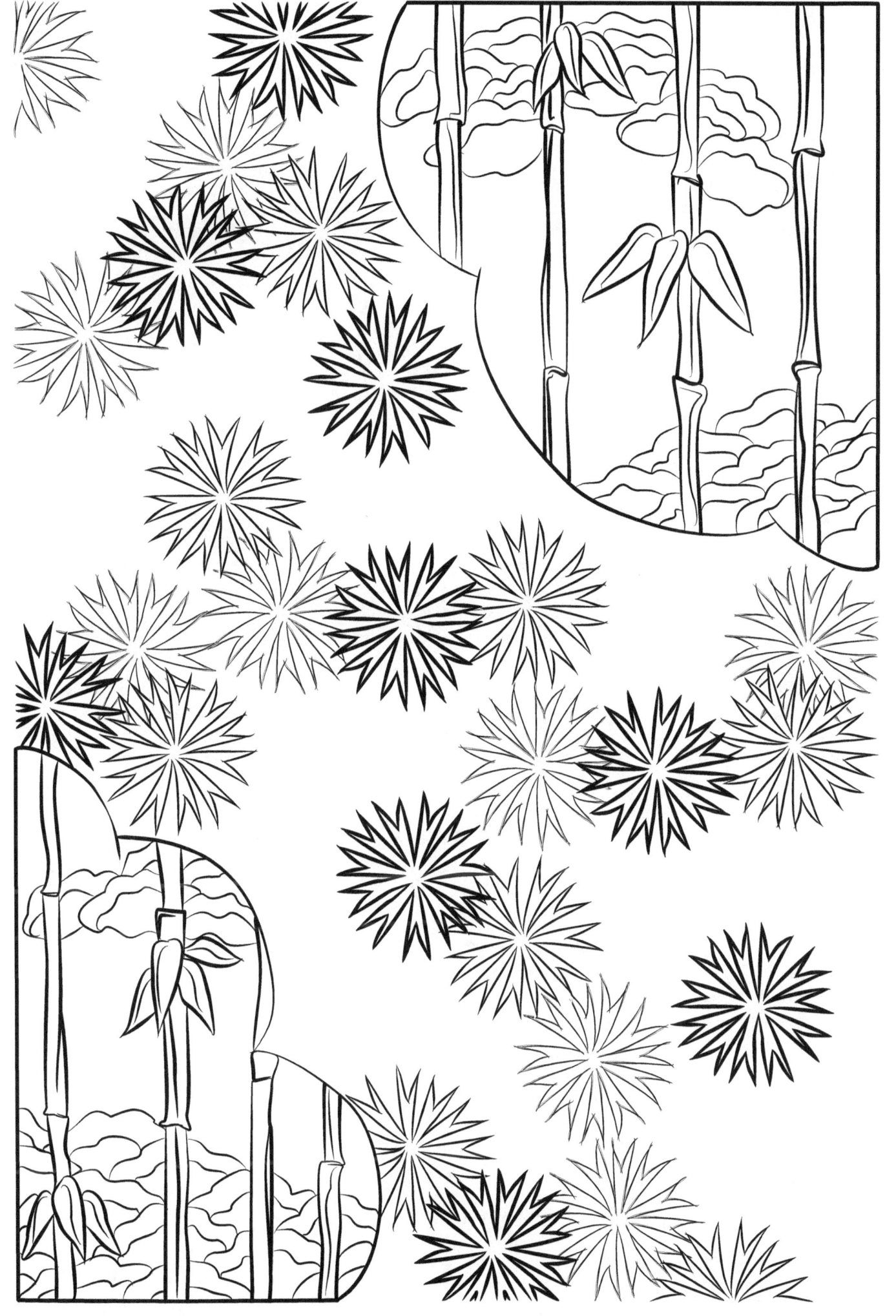

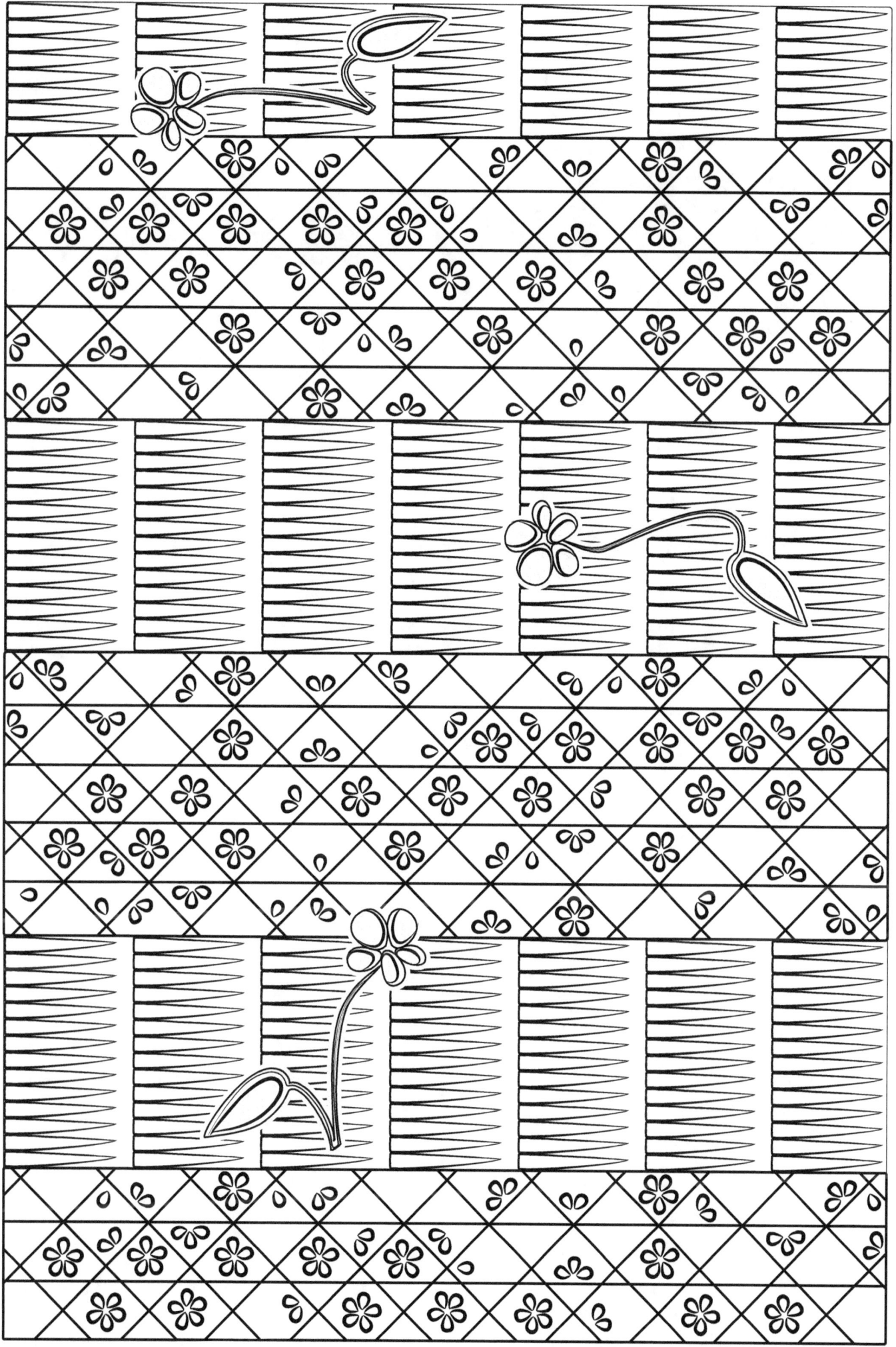

ArtworkAnywhere.com

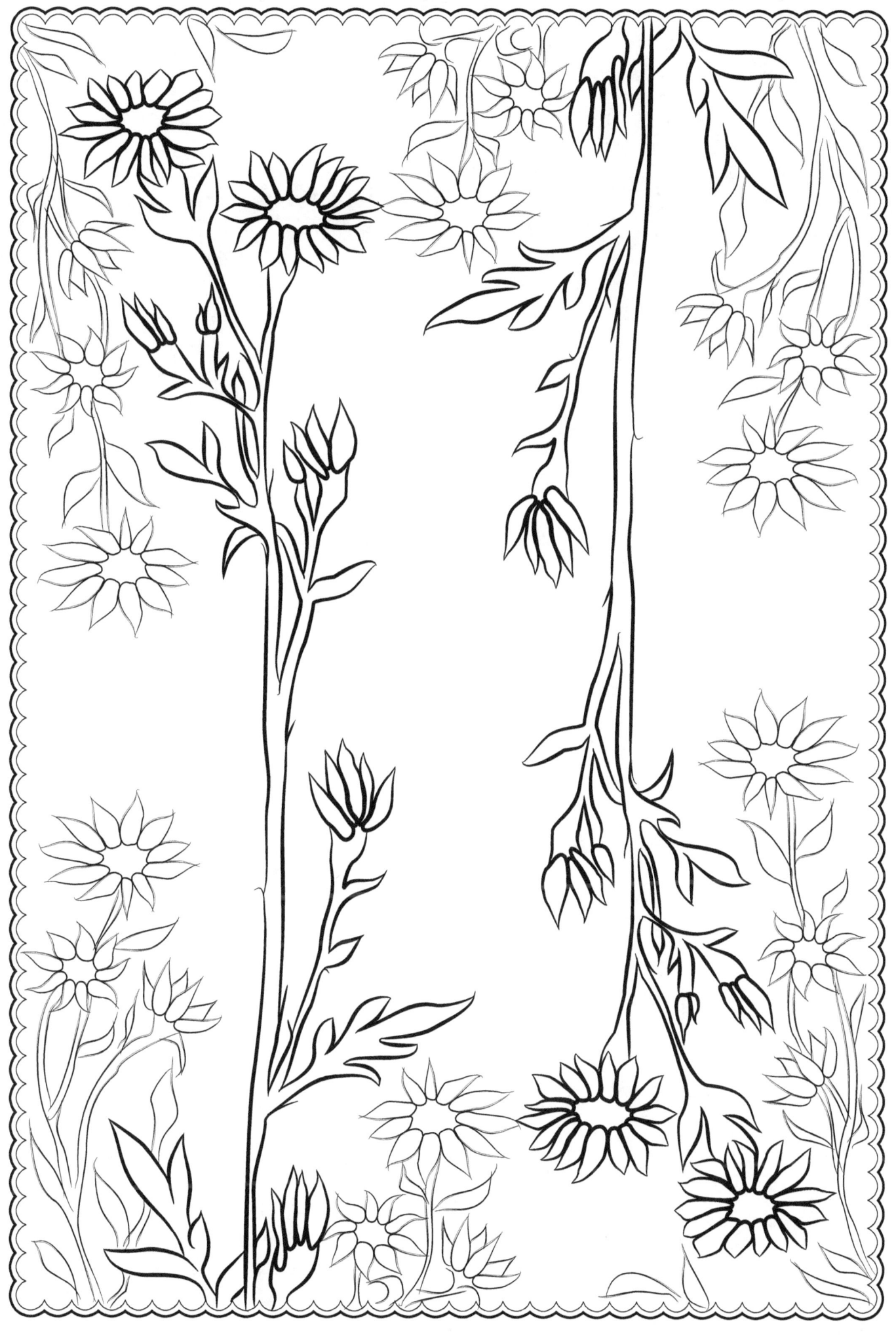

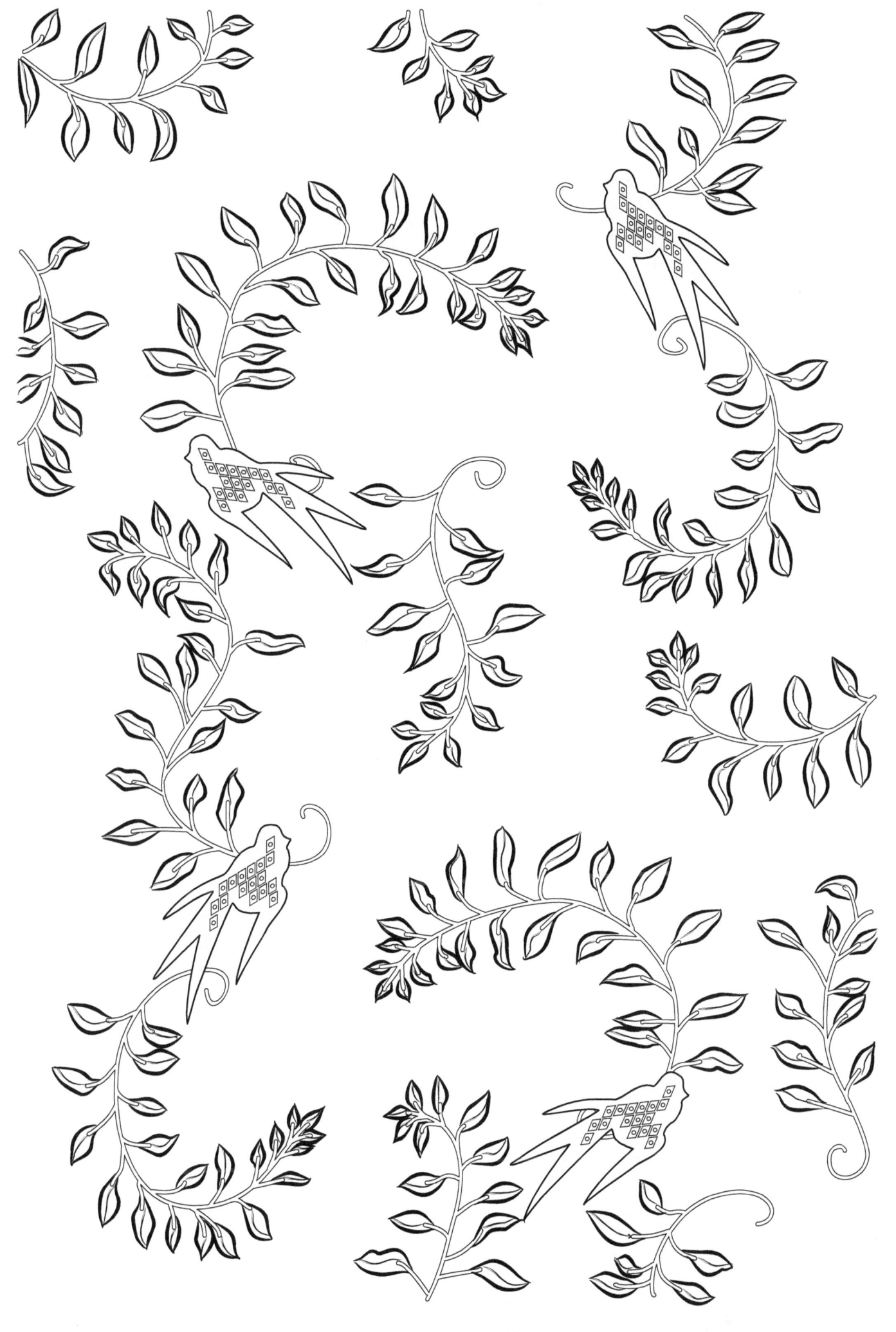

ArtworkAnywhere.com

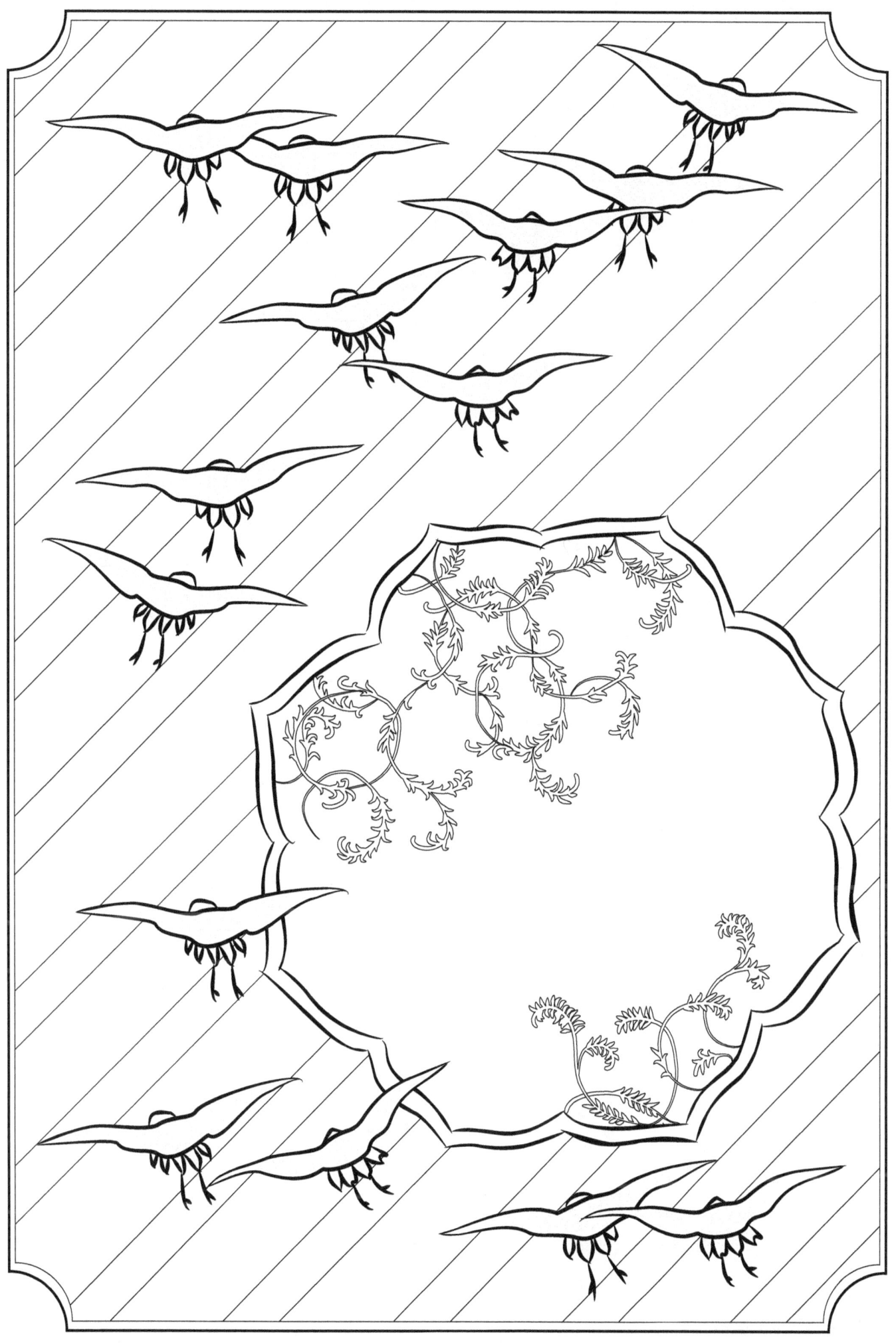

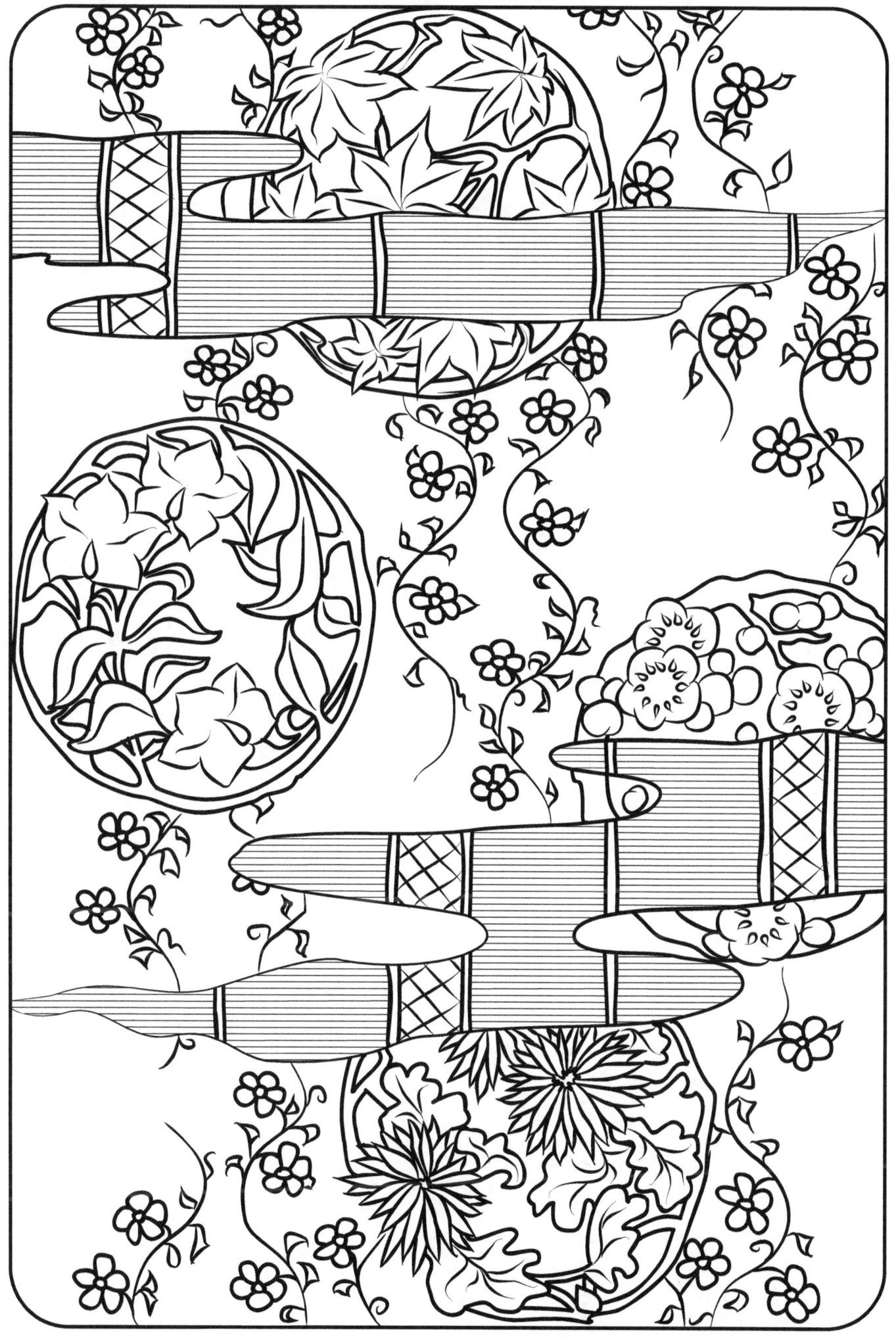

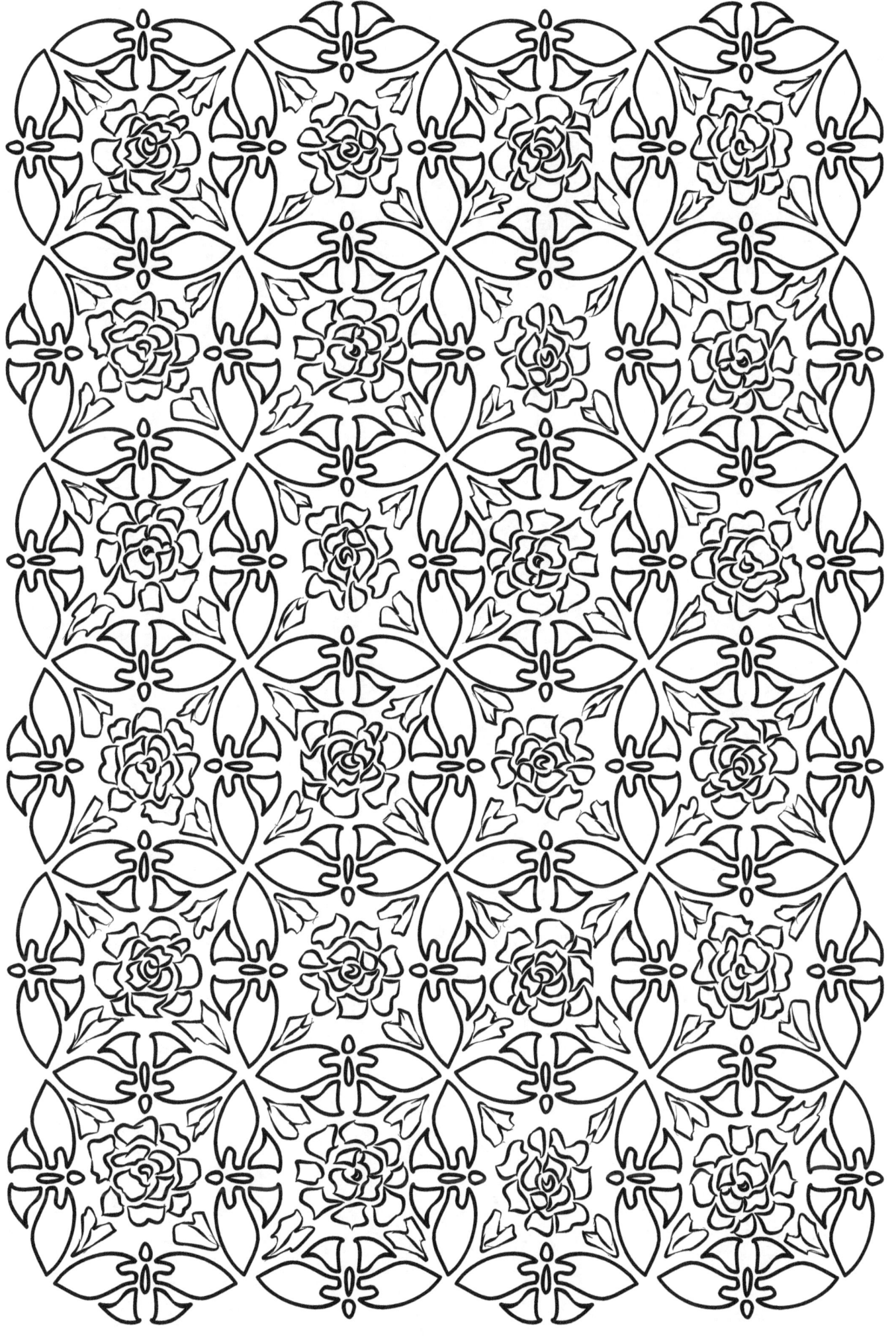

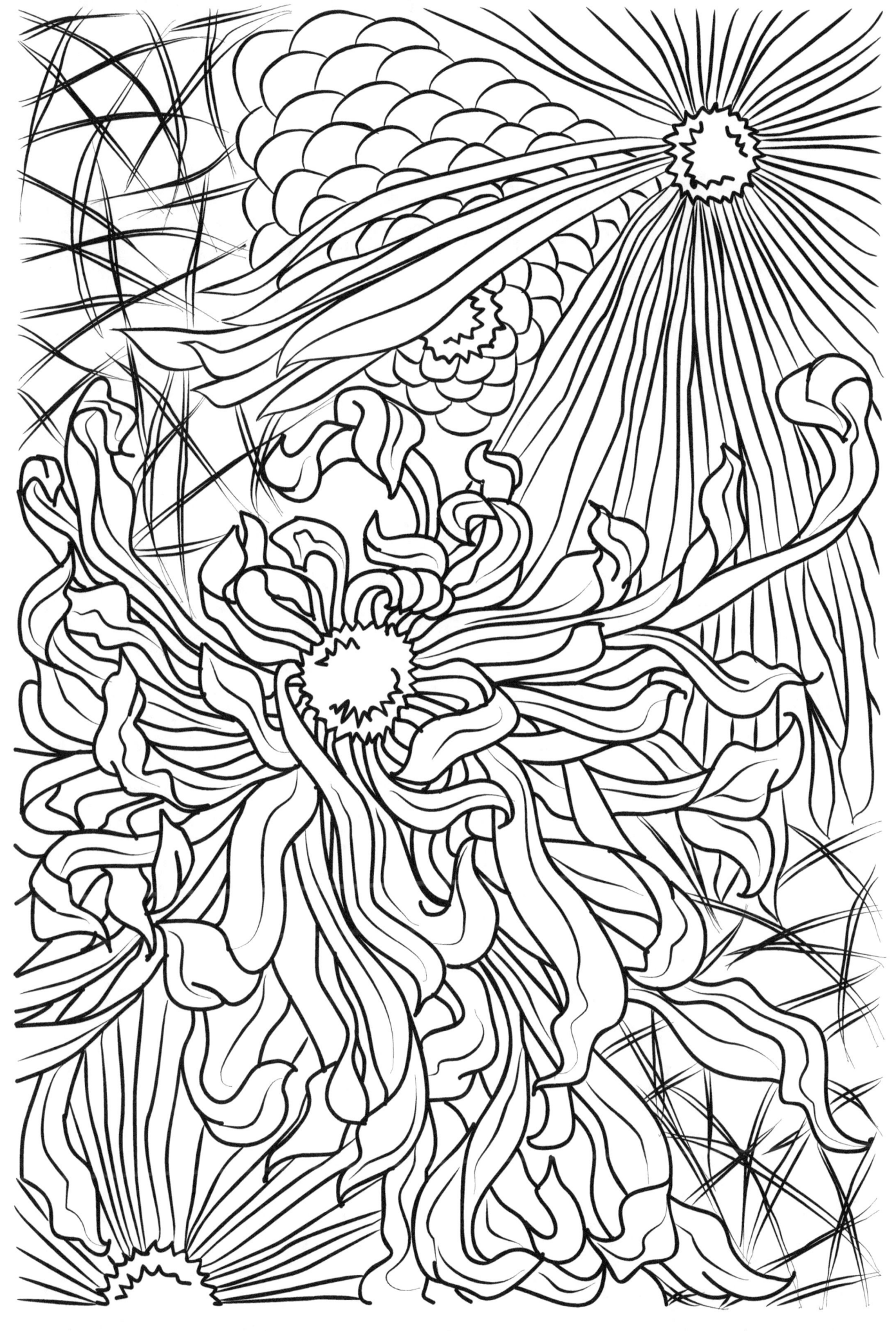

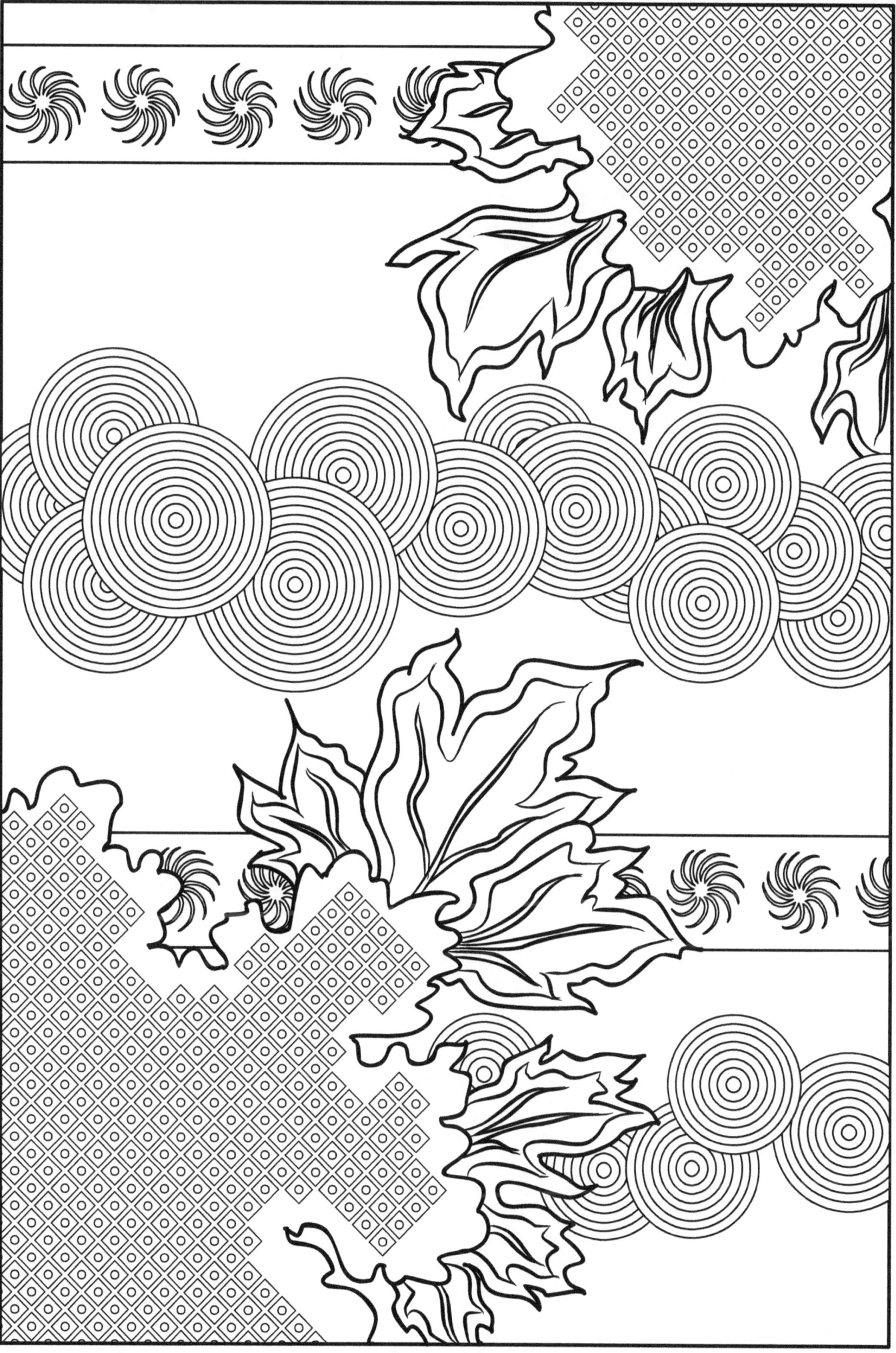

ArtworkAnywhere.com

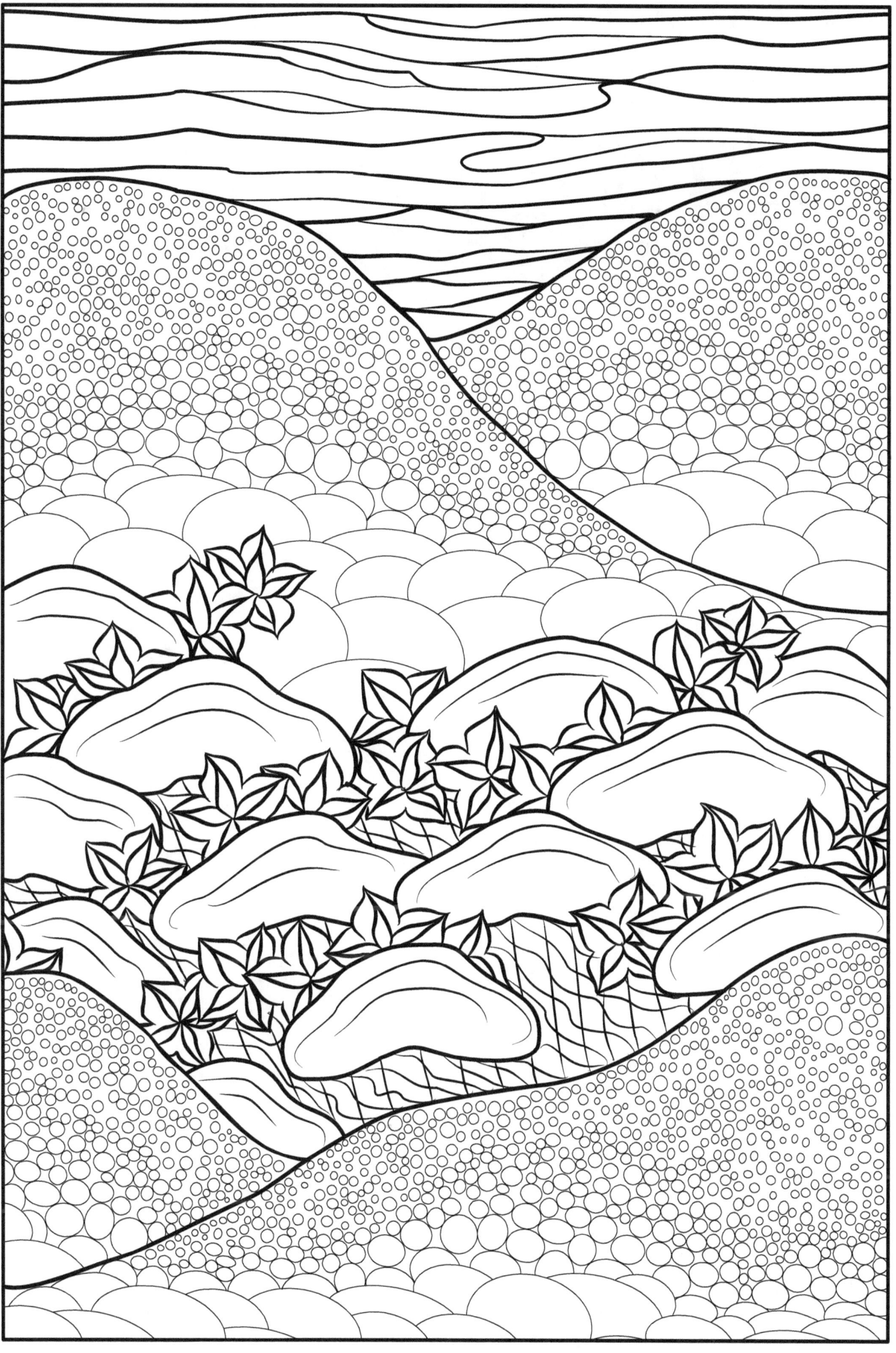

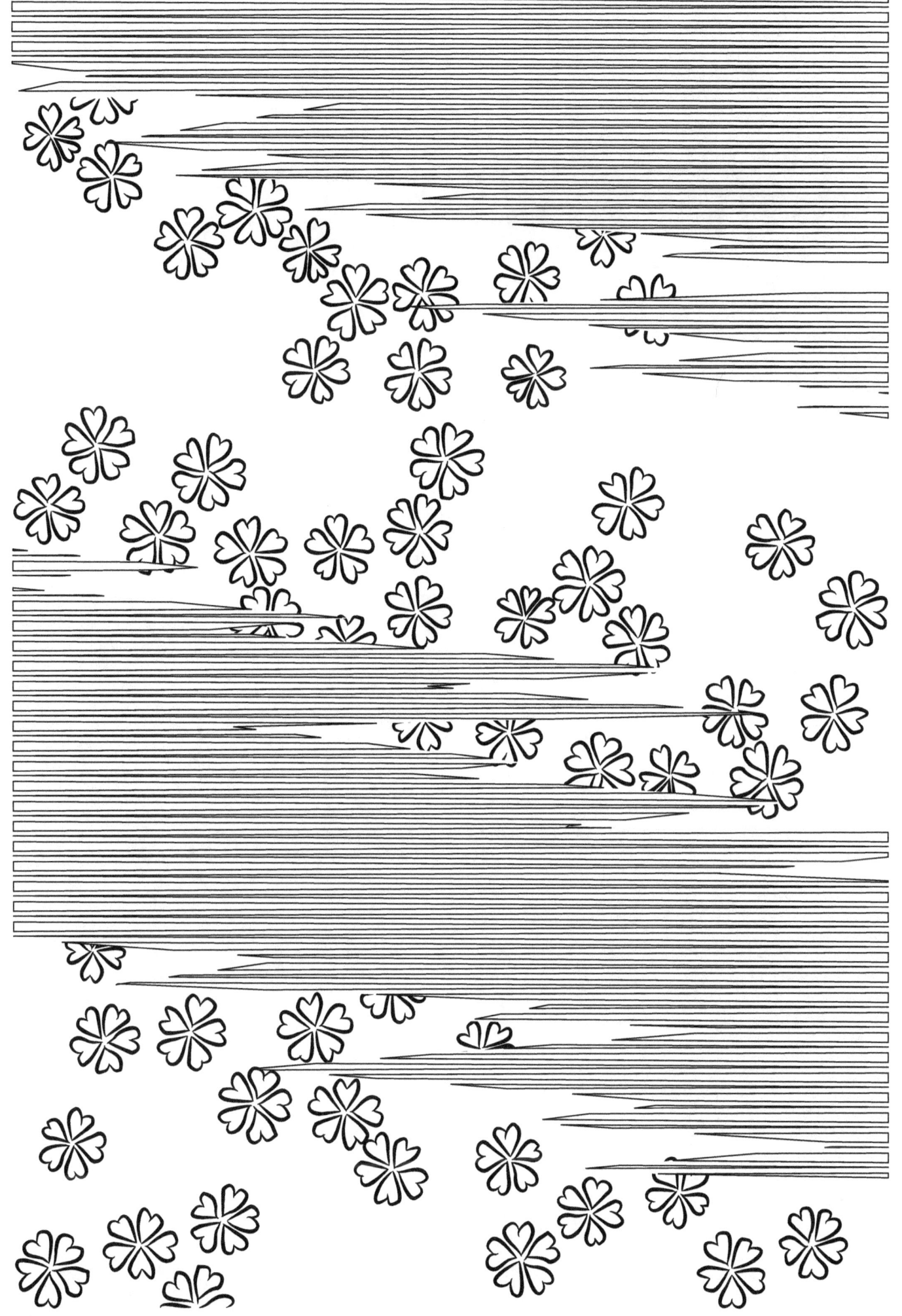

ArtworkAnywhere.com

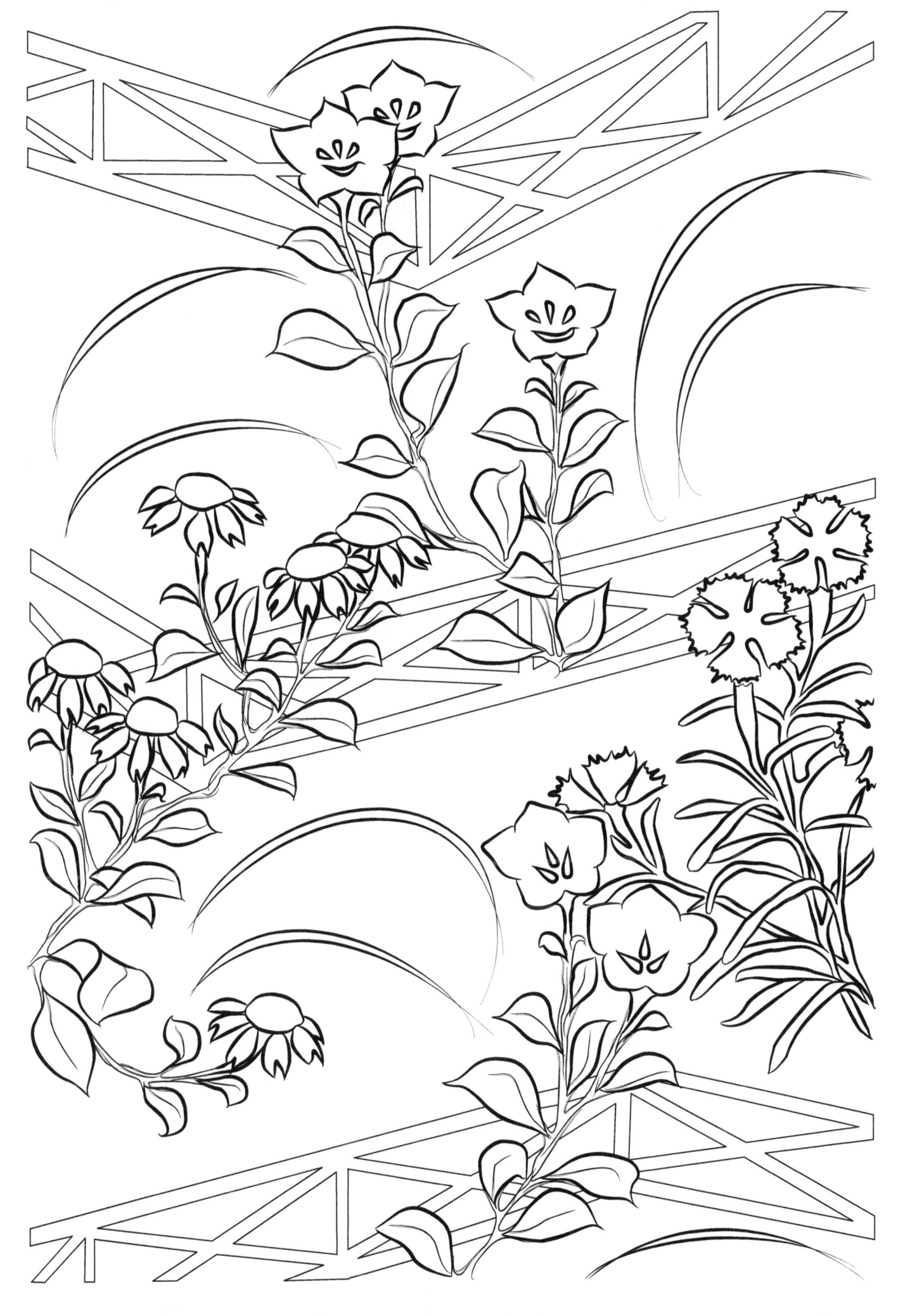

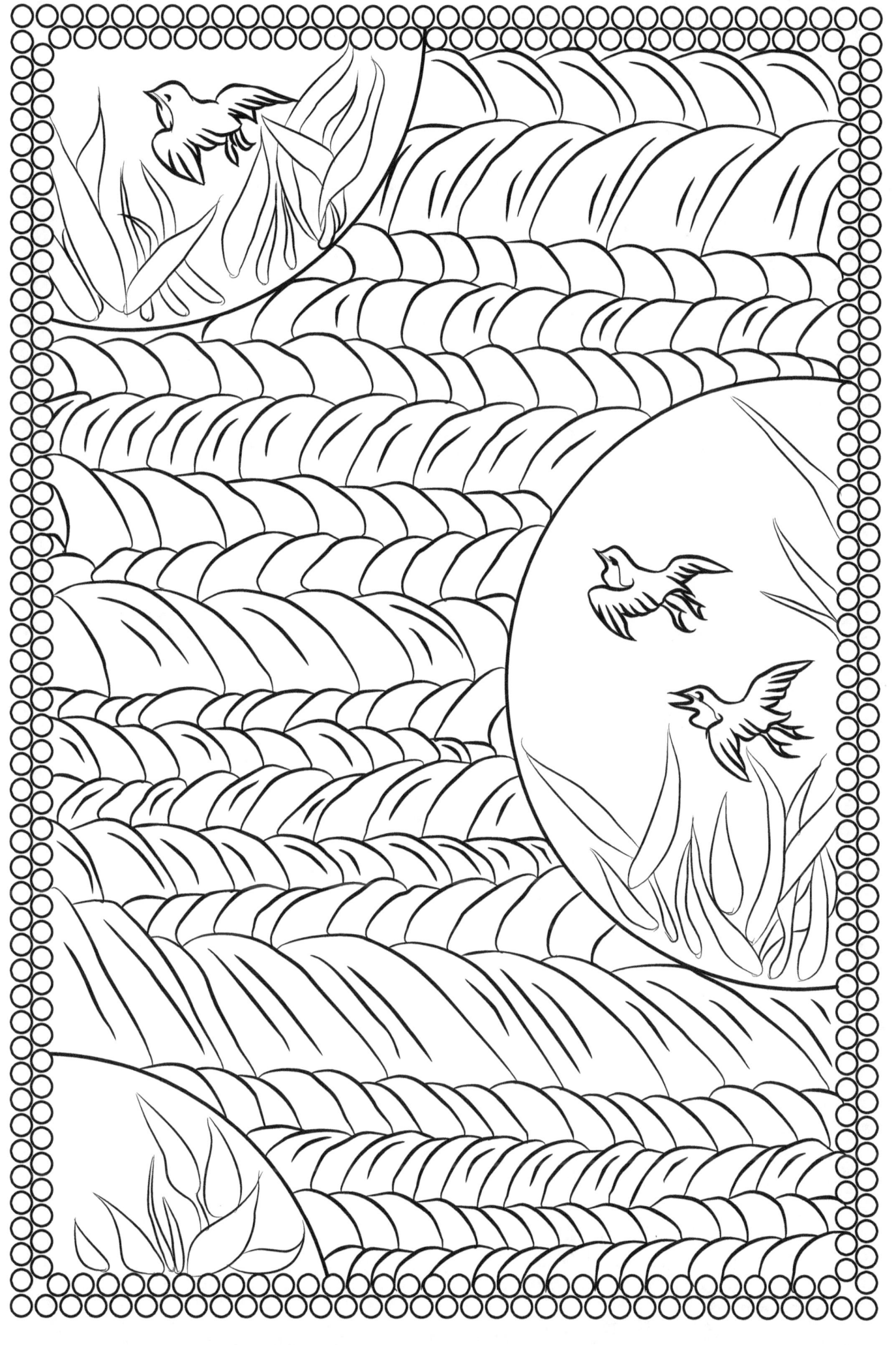

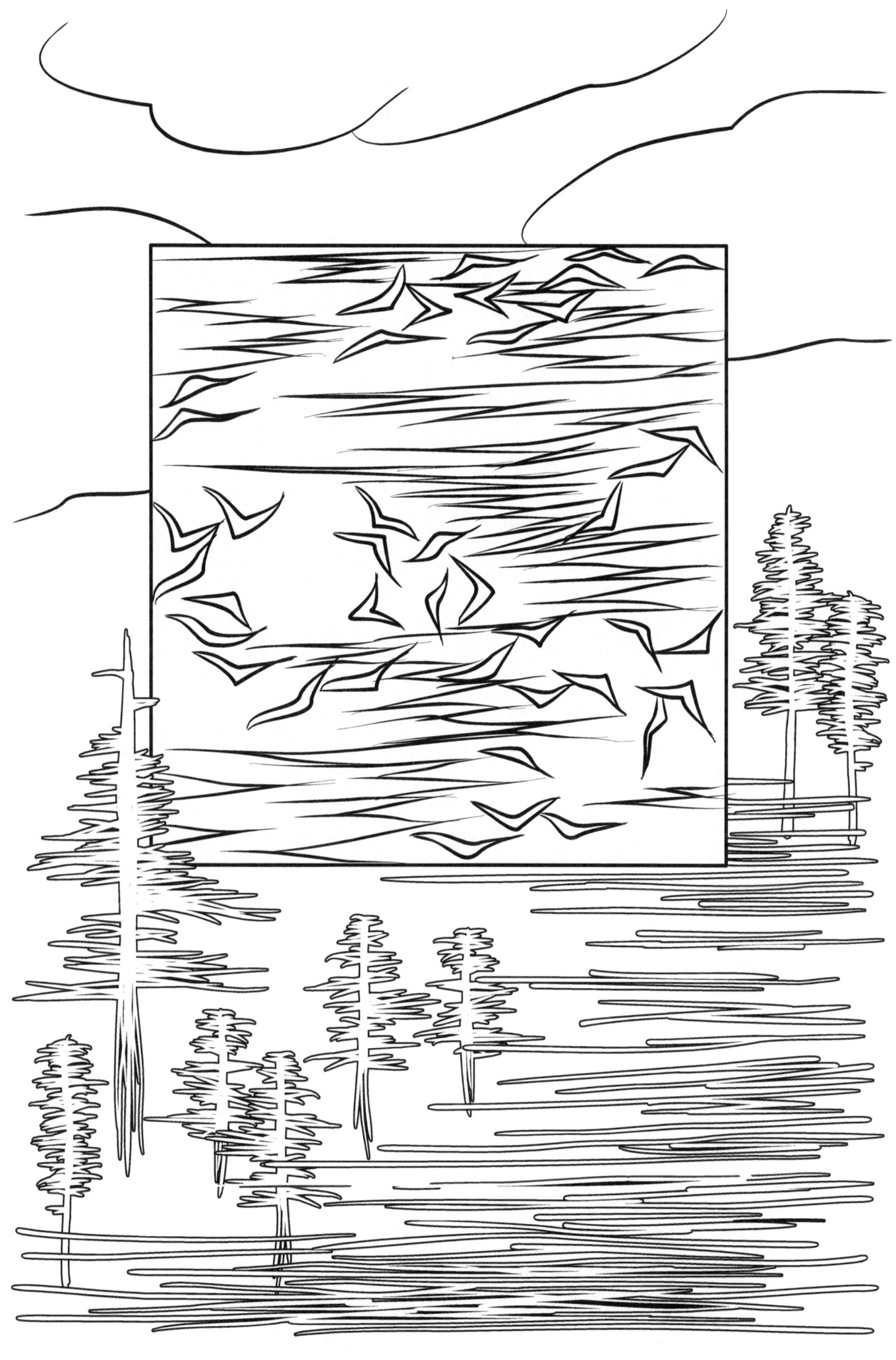

ArtworkAnywhere.com

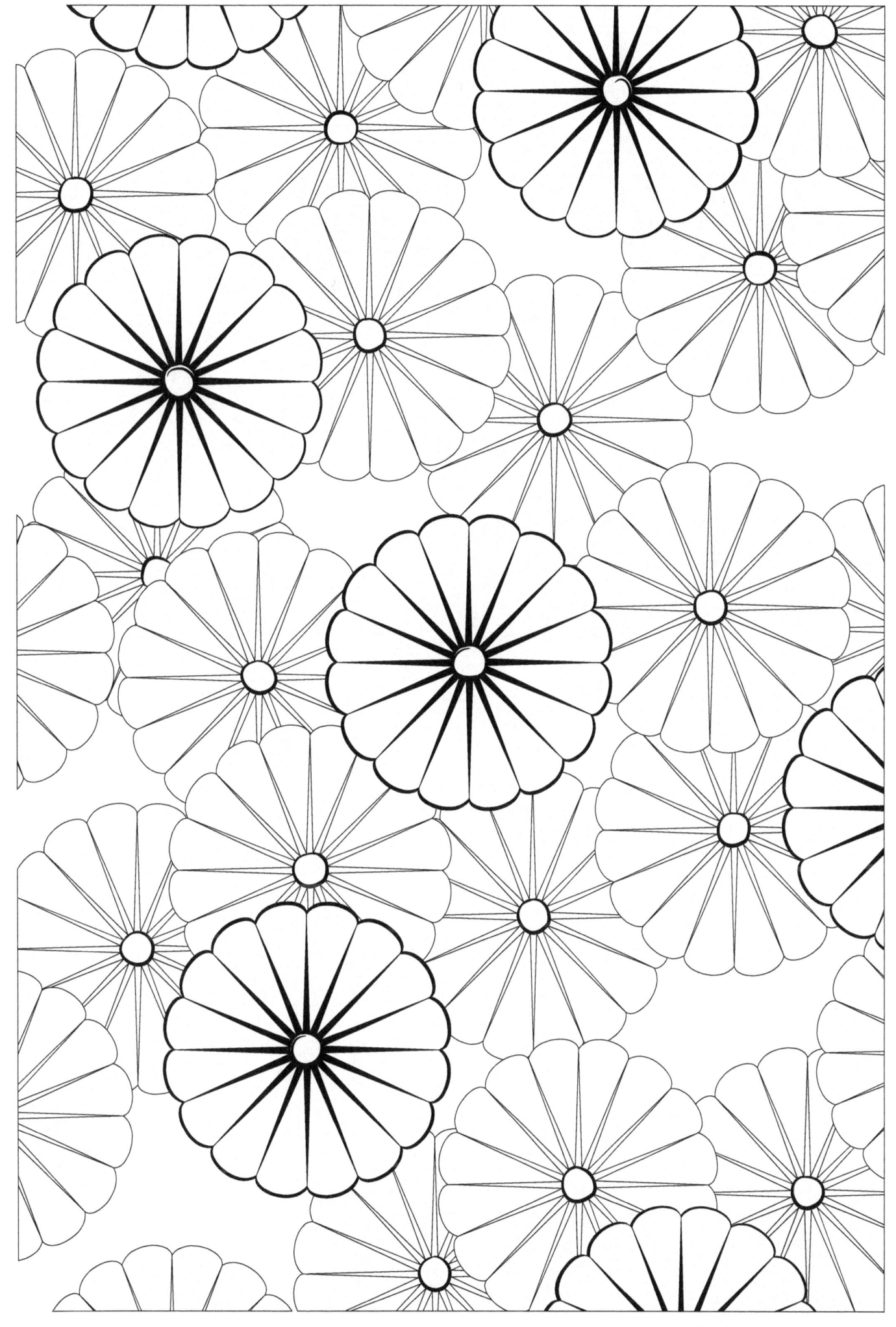

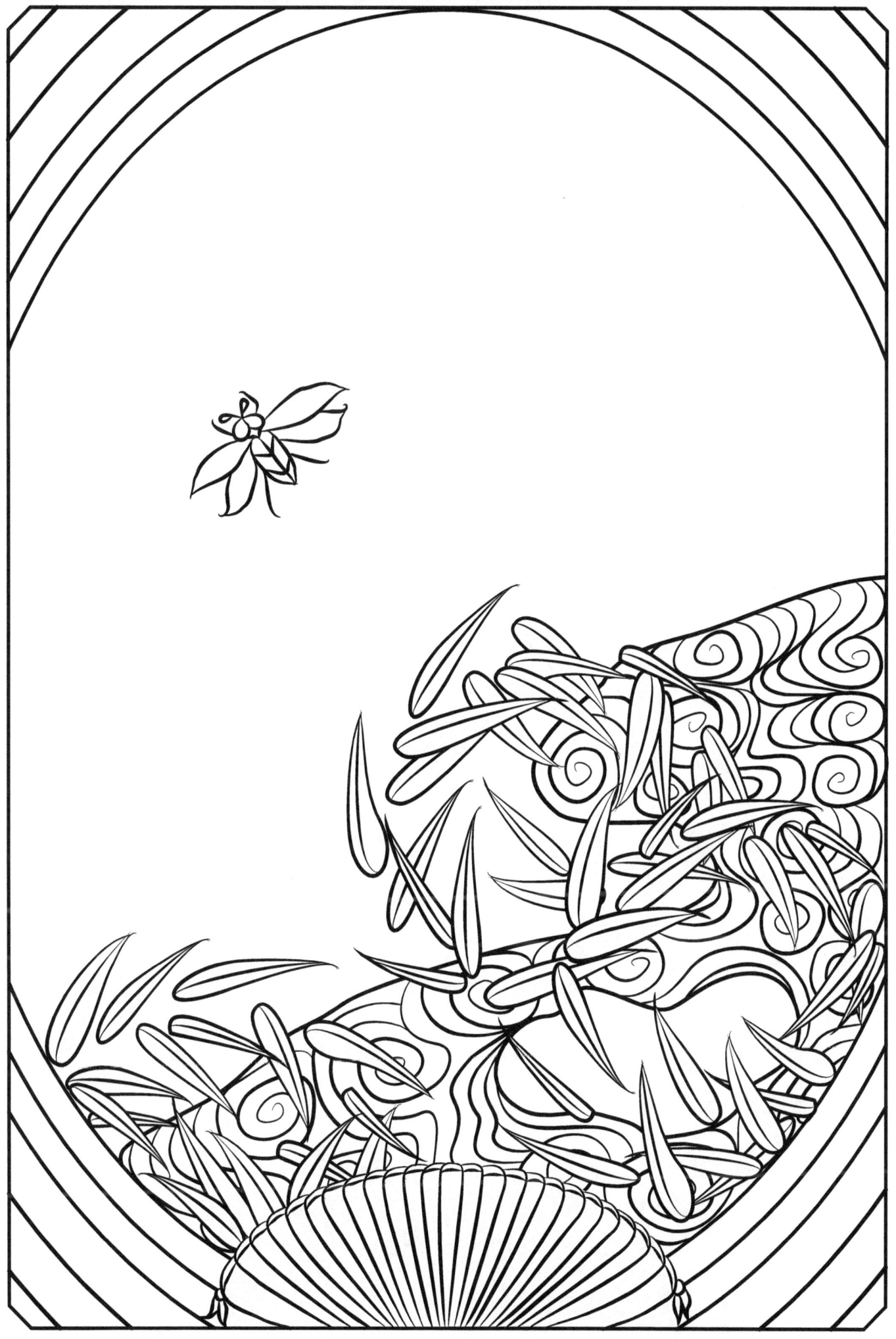

ArtworkAnywhere.com

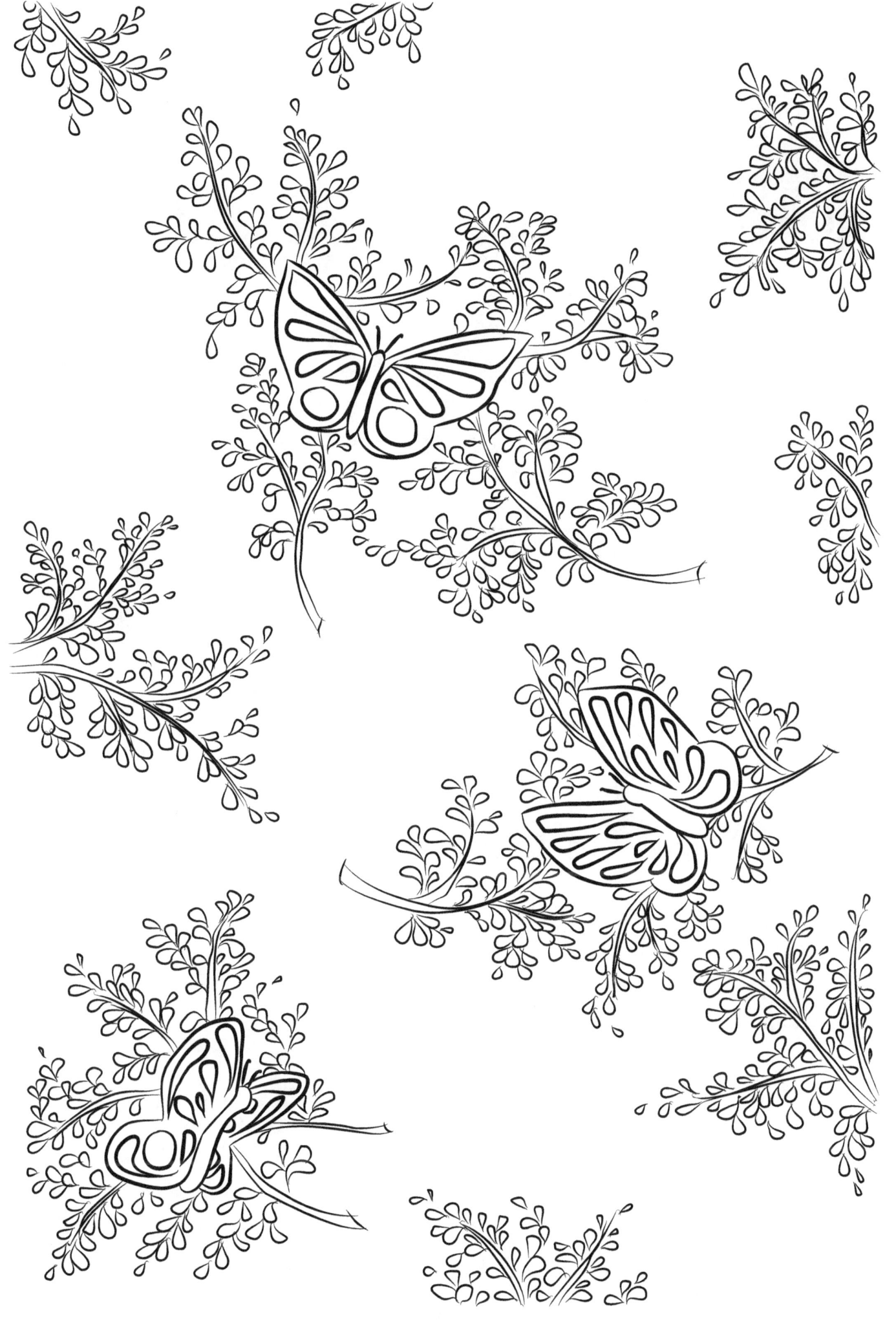

ArtworkAnywhere.com

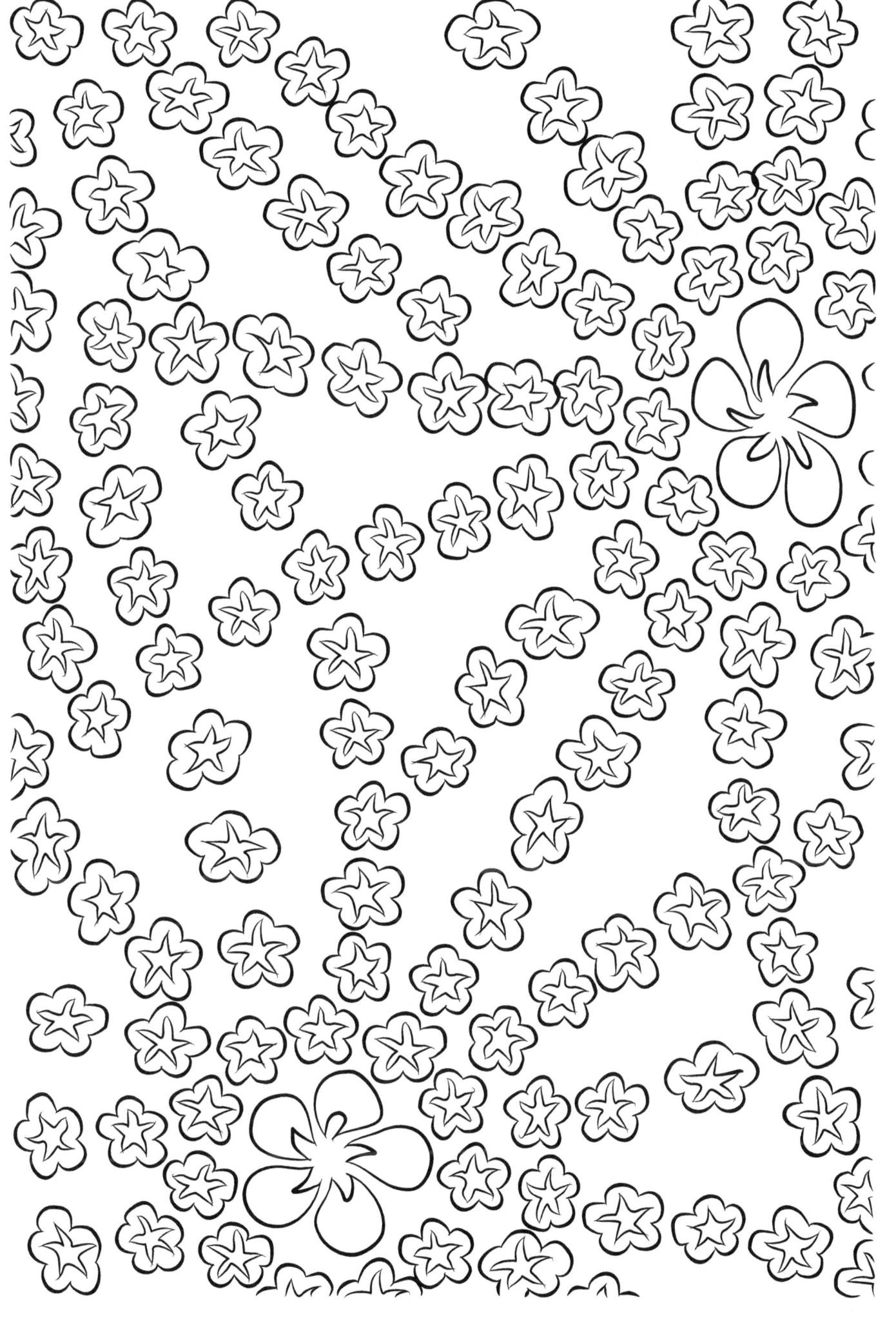

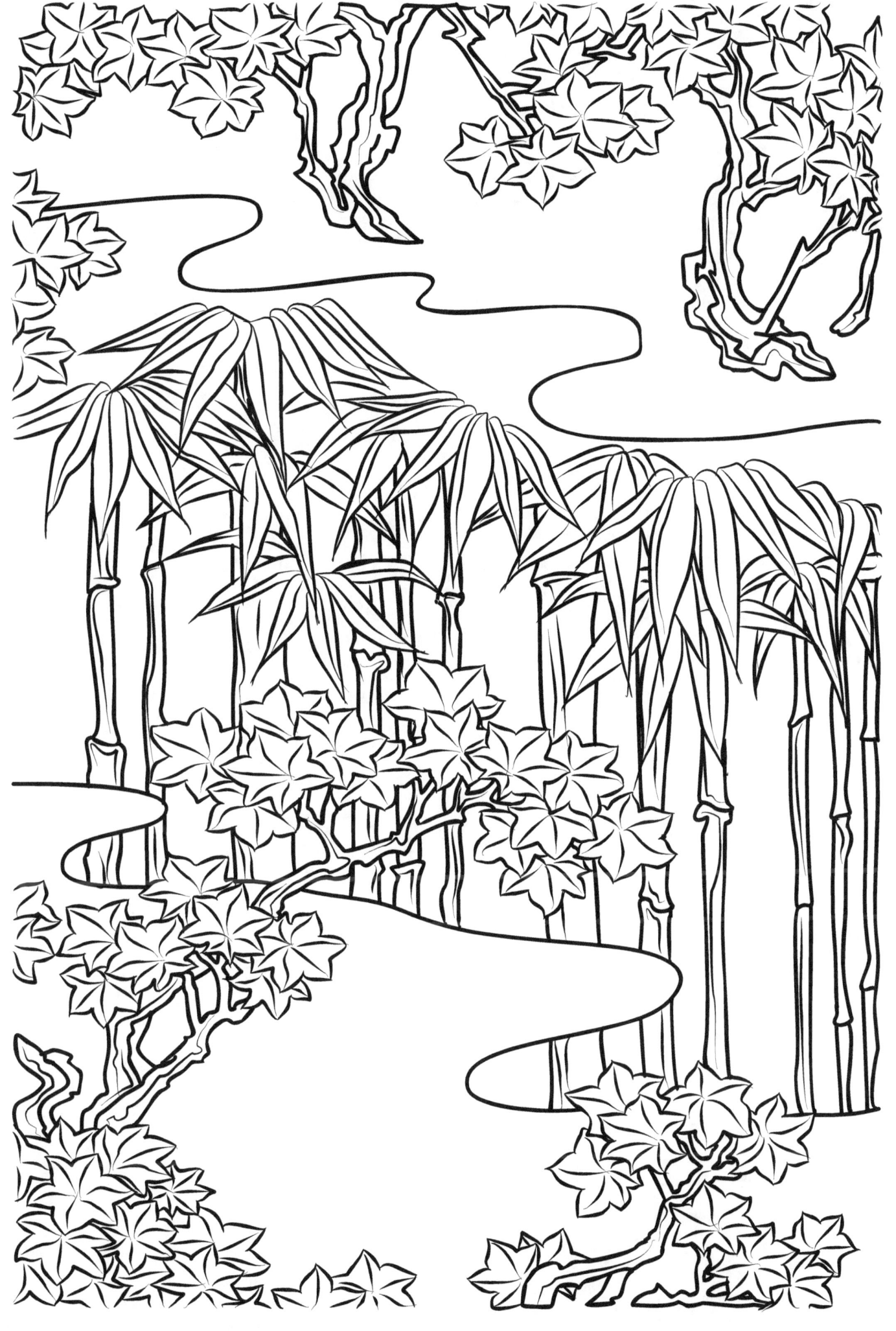

ArtworkAnywhere.com

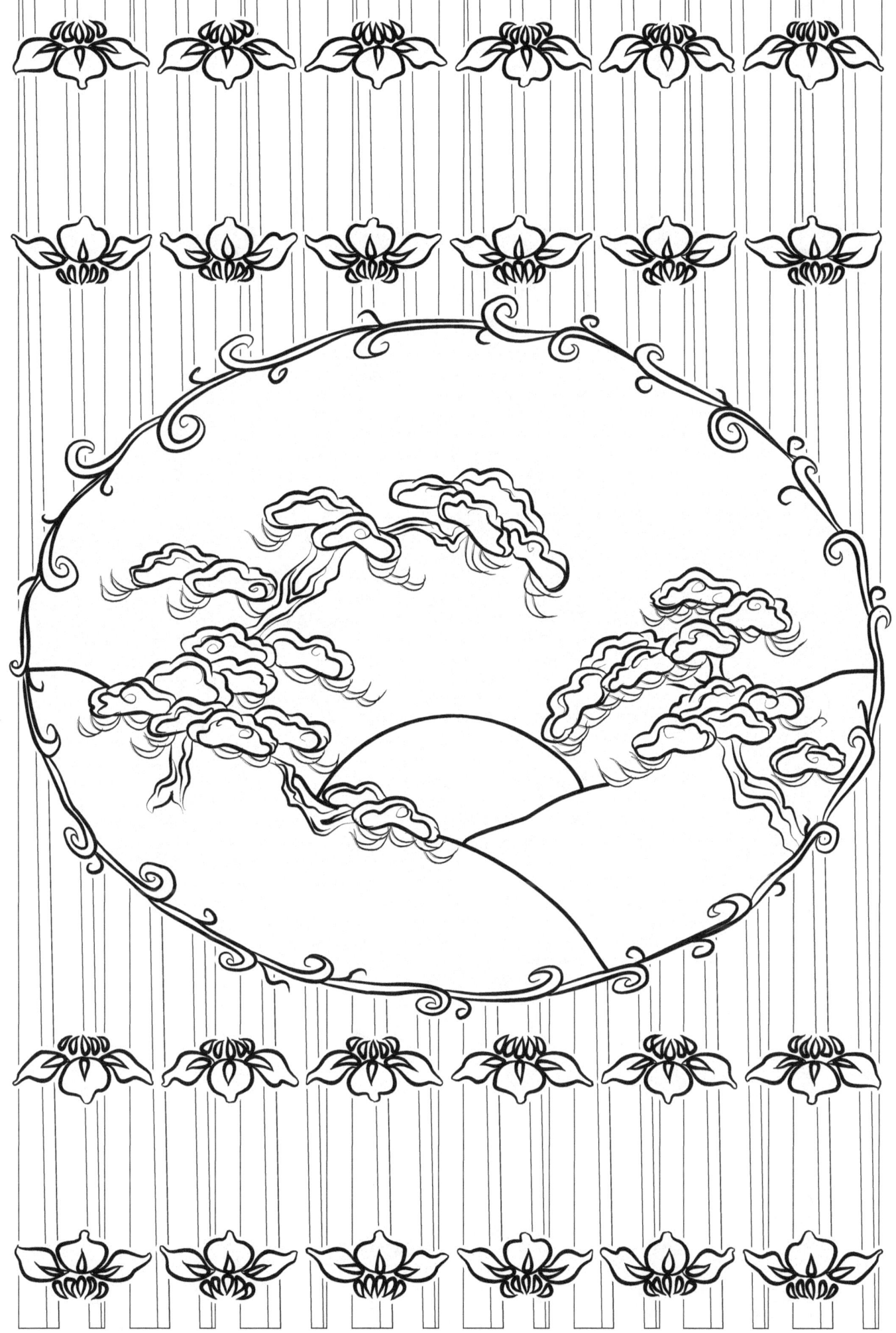

ArtworkAnywhere.com

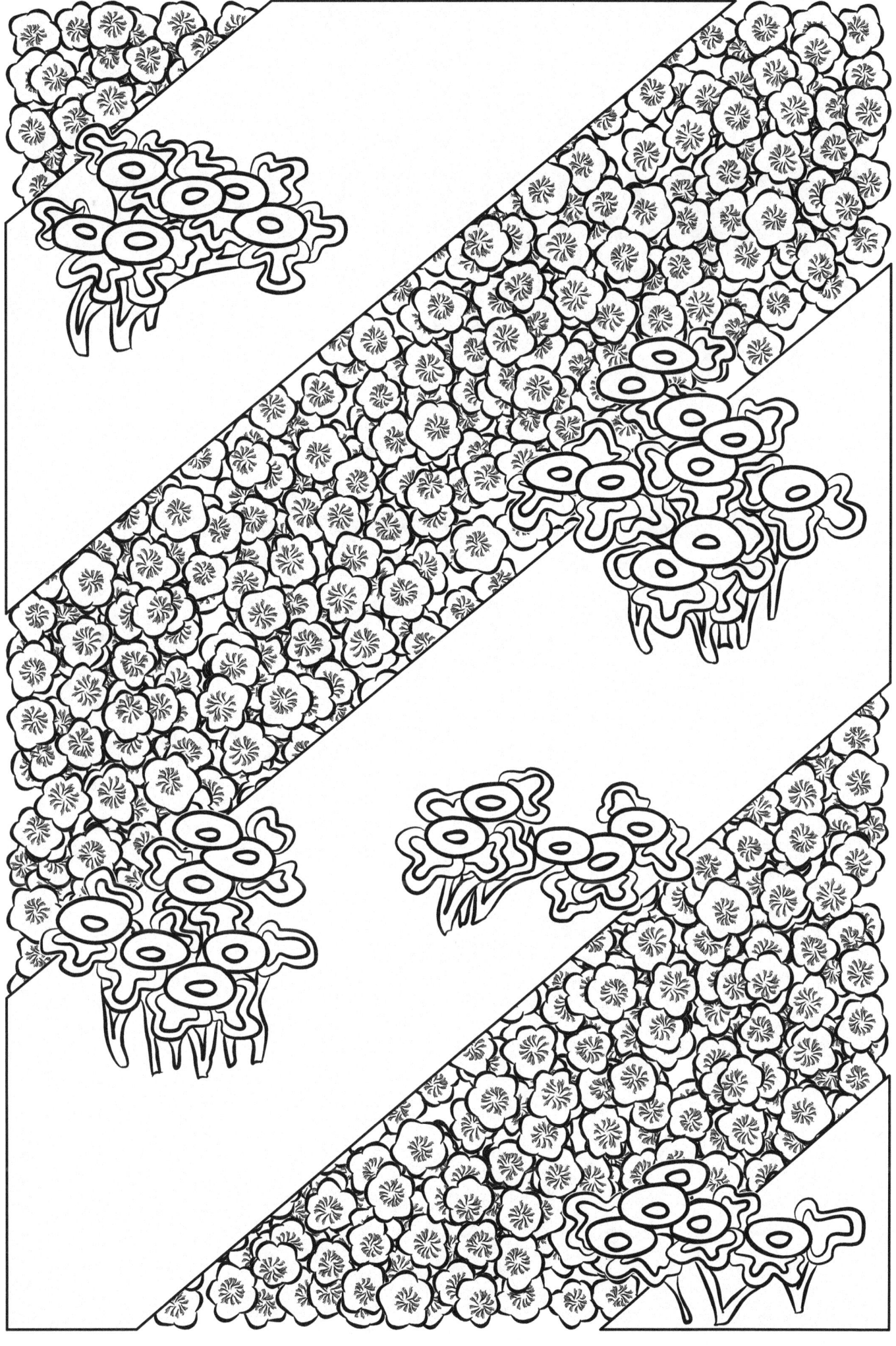

www.ingramcontent.com/pod-product-compliance
Lightning Source LLC
Chambersburg PA
CBHW080553190526
45169CB00007B/2761